THE BUSINESS
Diaries

10 Start-Up Secrets for the
Female Entrepreneur

Heather Hays

Copyright (C) 2024 Heather Hays

Heatherhays.co

All rights reserved. No part of this publication may be reproduced, distributed, stored in a retrieval system, or transmitted by any means, by recording or other electronic or mechanical methods, without the prior written permission of the author, except by reviewers who may quote brief passages in a review.

This publication is designed to provide accurate and authoritative information in regard to the subject matter covered. It is sold with the understanding that neither the author nor the publisher is engaged in rendering legal, investment, accounting, or other professional services. While the publisher and author have used their best efforts in preparing this book, they make no representations or warranties with respect to the accuracy or completeness of the contents of this book and specifically disclaim any implied warranties of merchantability or fitness for a particular purpose. No warranty may be created or extended by sales representatives or written sales materials. The advice and strategies contained herein may not be suitable for your situation. You should consult with a professional when appropriate. Neither the publisher nor the author shall be liable for any loss of profit or any other commercial damages, including but not limited to special, incidental, consequential, personal, or other damages.

Book Cover by Artist - Julie Pearl

Illustrator - Korina Verlance

First edition, 2024

For Madison & McKenzie.

You inspire me every day, and Palm Tree Playground was one of those wonderful ideas that would not have been possible without you.

I love you forever.

For Eric.

The best business and life partner.

I love you always.

For my mom and sister.

Thank you for believing I can do things even when I can't.

I love you two and a half hearts forever.

For my friends.

Thank you for walking alongside me knowing my secret and loving me through it. You know who you are.

And for the Palm Tree Playground Team.

Thank you to our amazing managers. Everything was possible because of you.

To our excellent party hosts, you made children smile and parents relax to help create memories for a lifetime.

You all will always have a huge place in the Hays family's heart.

The Business Diaries Bonus Secrets

This "diary" is full of entrepreneurial secrets, and the first one is a secret gift!

Head over to heatherhays.co/book and download your free bonus bundle with action items, planning worksheets, and journal prompts.

Contents

Introduction 1

Secret One: Your Business Plan Needs to Reflect Your Life Plan 9

    How to Find a Business Concept 9
    20 Questions to Simplify Writing Your Business Plan . 13
    It's OK to Start Small 18

Secret Two: Don't Fund Your Loan Too Soon 25

    You Want Me to Wait to Fund My Loan? 26
    What Went Wrong 30
    What Could Have Gone Right 32

Secret Three: You Are Not Alone: Create a Team, Use the App, and Identify Your Power Players 37

    Create a Team NOW 38
    Use the App! 42
    Identify Your Power Players 47

Secret Four: Popularity Doesn't Always Equal Profitability 51

    Brand Awareness 52
    Make an Offer 54
    Metrics and Key Performance Indicators 56

Secret Five: Make Salespeople Your Business Partners 61

    Salespeople Can Add or Take Away from Your Business 61
    Sales Empowerment List 65
    Sales Partnership Questionnaire 67

Secret Six: Bad Clients Teach and Good Clients Preach....75

    The Bad Client............75
    The Good Client............79
    How to Show Client Appreciation............80

Secret Seven: Volunteer with Purpose............85

    Lack of Success Substitution............85
    Volunteer with Purpose............87

Secret Eight: Self-Care Is Good Business............97

    You Don't Want the Urgent Matter to Be You............97
    12 Ideas to Get Healthier Today............100

Secret Nine: Invest in Yourself: Find a Mentor, Sales Training, or Entrepreneurship Program............105

    Why You Need a Mentor, Training, or Program............105
    How Sales Training Can Help You............111
    Overcoming "I Don't Have Time"............112

Secret Ten: You Can (Sometimes) Sell a Business that Isn't Profitable............117

    How to Find a Buyer for Your Business............117
    Information Requested by Potential Buyers............119
    Life After the Business Sale............122

Conclusion............127

INTRODUCTION

I have a secret, and some of my friends don't even know what it is all these years later. Since you are interested in this book, I am going to assume three things:

The first is that you might have a similar secret.

The second is that you are an entrepreneur.

The third, and final, is that you are in one of three predicaments:

1. You just opened your business;
2. You just closed your business; or
3. You are in the process of figuring out what to do with your business.

Entrepreneurship comes with many positive attributes like ownership, innovation, resilience, a flexible schedule but it also means long hours and late nights, total fiscal responsibility, no set income and possible failure. Despite the uncertainty, entrepreneurship continues to entice people everyday.

An entrepreneur exudes creativity, courage, and endless optimism while risking everything to bring a new product or idea to market. It can be absolutely exhilarating. Then that product is judged by everyone to decide if the idea is good or bad, interesting or boring, and whether or not it will be a success or failure.

My obsession with owning my own business started in fifth grade, and regardless of all my creative pursuits, having my own business was always a goal.

When I turned thirty-seven, I made that goal a reality. I hired twelve team members, invested $400,000, and eventually won awards for my establishment. Palm Tree Playground, an indoor paradise for parties and playdates, became a popular place for one- to five-year-olds to celebrate birthdays, and moms' groups hosted all types of events there. We even had our own summer camp.

While running our business, I received emails from other entrepreneurs monthly. All the messages were the same. They all asked for advice on how to start a business, get a loan, find an amazing group of employees, set up payroll, find play equipment, design ads, and create a solid reputation in the community.

Sometimes I was brutally honest about finances, and other times I didn't want to ruin their excitement and sugarcoated it. I did offer straight talk all the time because my information might give them a better business model to work from and more success than I was experiencing. That is what I hope this book will do for you.

Every time I received an email, I felt excited about the notion that my business had reached the radar of another person who loves the creation of a new business as much as I do. And then my second thought would always be, "But this person doesn't know my secret: I feel like a fraud, and worse yet, I feel like a liar."

Only my closest friends were let in on the biggest disappointment of my career: my successful business was an utter failure in that it made very little profit.

We had so many wins and happy clients, so only a few people knew the absolute ego-shattering, humbling, anxiety-producing disappointments that were happening behind the scenes.

Today, there are many inspirational books that tell you if you work hard enough, you will attain your dreams. They usually acknowledge there will be setbacks, but the underlying message is, "Work hard and gain success." I truly believed this, so I wore myself into the ground chasing a business that wasn't meant to be mine. Yes, I had dreamed it up and gotten it started, but maybe I wasn't meant to run it forever. Maybe creating it was enough? Perhaps I didn't succeed because there was something better for me to chase after or maybe there was something I didn't need to chase at all? Sometimes you work hard and it doesn't work.

So why on earth would you ever buy a book about a failed business venture? I have turned my one secret of failure into ten secrets of success. I want you to know that you are not alone in this entrepreneurial endeavor. You might be in a start-up phase and these secrets can potentially save you thousands of dollars. I wish I had known these ten secrets, and I am determined that you will. Business classes can't always give you the real-life details that are the difference between making it and breaking it. Finally, perhaps you are trying to sell your business and you have been told no one will invest in it. I was in that position and ended up selling it regardless. I didn't get rich, but I did manage to pay off a large portion of my debt.

While I ran my start-up, the same criticism popped into my head every time I worried about payroll or I had to use the company card to pay the energy bill: "Why did I do this to myself?"

The answer hit me when I walked through the glass doors of my little slice of the American dream: I absolutely loved what my husband and I had created. If I could go back and answer the emails I received, this book is how I would do it, this sneak peek of entrepreneurial real life. This is what business owners don't tell you because it doesn't look good on an Instagram feed or might make people judge them. It's a deep dive into the successes that made up Palm Tree Playground and the missteps that almost tore it down.

The amazing part of my story is that despite all my challenges, the business sold to an interested party when I could no longer invest more energy into it. Most business schools will tell you that in order to sell a business, you have to show profit for two or more years. So how did we sell to an accomplished buyer who wasn't passionate about Palm Tree Playground like I was? I will tell you at the end of this book. We will chat about how we built it, sold it, and thrived through the ups and downs of the entrepreneurial wave of life and how you can too.

I am spilling my secrets so you can be successful. My top ten are as follows:

1. Your Business Plan Should Reflect Your Life Plan
2. Don't Fund Your Loan Too Soon
3. You Are Not Alone
4. Popularity Doesn't Always Equal Profitability
5. Make Salespeople Your Business Partners
6. Bad Clients Teach and Good Clients Preach
7. Volunteer with Purpose
8. Self-Care Is Good Business
9. Invest in Yourself
10. You Can (Sometimes) Sell a Business that Isn't Profitable

I will illustrate how these start-up secrets can save you time, money, and peace of mind. I'm opening up my business diaries because I believe if we all share entrepreneurial knowledge and experience, we all win.

An entrepreneur exudes creativity, courage and endless optimism while risking everything to bring a new product or idea to market.

Secret One

YOUR BUSINESS PLAN NEEDS TO REFLECT YOUR LIFE PLAN

How to Find a Business Concept

A computer hacker had on a black hoodie, tight jeans, and headphones blasting toe-tapping music. His casual attire directly contrasted the rich paneled walnut walls that shone from the computer's glare. The plush, tufted leather sofa sat in the corner on top of a luxurious gold carpet. His Adidas sneakers sank into the overpriced weave as he hunched over his laptop while dancing his fingers across the keys.

He had limited time to find the banking file needed to transfer $100 million from this Wall Street business tycoon to the charity the wealthy man tried to steal from just months ago. The numbers were racing across the screen while the bank account balance lowered and the charity's account rose. The seconds ticked off, 30, then 20—just a few more needed before the security guard once again peeked into the office suite that looked more like a luxury condo than a workplace. The hacker had a bead of sweat on his top lip and wiped it with the back of his leather-gloved right hand just as the transfer completed.

"Cut," yelled the director. "Back to one. Taking it again from the top."

My husband was the first assistant director on season two of a television show filming in Portland, Oregon, and they were filming a similar scene. I was drenched because it was raining again, but I loved bringing our almost three-year-old and four-month-old daughters to the set to visit Eric while on location. That's why we were in Portland in the first place!

It was May, and out of the past nine weeks we had been here, it had rained forty-nine of the days. After the set visit, I loaded our daughters into my Toyota Sequoia and headed to the promised land of motherhood. Well, it was really a nursery school that opened for 2 one-hour sessions during the week and offered playtime to anyone under five years old. I had seen the flier in a strip mall and marked my calendar a week in advance. The diaper bag was packed with snacks and changes of clothes, the rain jackets were on, and we were off and ready to enjoy this walk-in play hour.

Previously our family had been kicked out of the library. Our three-year-old cutie couldn't comprehend sitting next to children without talking to, poking, or hugging them.

The amazing children's museum was downtown, and there was just not enough time between naps and dinner to get our money's worth. But this indoor play area with slides and dress-up clothes, ball pits and books, well, it was heaven.

This was my new weekly routine. I paid $5 to let my older daughter, Madison, play for an hour while McKenzie slept in her car seat near me.

Then one day the play area pulled out all the stops and offered free steaming-hot coffee. It was at that exact moment I said to myself, "If we ever settle down in one city, I am opening an indoor playground."

The film business is finicky. One day everyone is living the dream life in LA, California, and the next day LA means Louisiana. So like all our film friends, we packed up our Southern California life and moved to the South.

I loved it. The people, the food, and the architecture quintessential to the region were inviting. New Orleans was exciting and always an adventure. And spoiler alert—it was even better now that we had kids!

My husband could work on film and TV shows and actually live in our house. And we could have him around and build a life. I was settled, but why was that not settling for me? Something was missing. My need to create a niche for myself was strongly urging me forward again. I wanted to dig in and create a business now that we had stopped moving around the country chasing film sets, and New Orleans is a wonderful start-up community rich with opportunity.

And then, the little Lake Oswego memory popped into my head. This was it! I was going to build a business from the ground up, offer a wonderful work environment for my team, provide a high-quality product to my customers, and reap the rewards of risking it all. I was going to create an indoor playground, beach style, in the Big Easy.

20 Questions to Simplify Writing Your Business Plan

Once I had my business idea, I needed money to finance it, and to obtain a bank loan, I needed a business plan. I estimated that my start-up costs would be in the $280,000 range, and we would finance a portion of that amount. There are incredibly helpful online programs that you can use to format your ideas into a cohesive narrative to either obtain a loan or just for your mental clarity. Search for "small business plan" or "write a business plan" to begin. Even if you don't need to raise capital, its useful to chart out your ideas to ensure your plan is viable.

I knew how to write, but I had no idea how to communicate the financial information necessary to get a banker's attention. Through research, I found a fantastic company called LivePlan, which we used for our Palm Tree Playground business plan. The reports they provide are not only comprehensive and attractive, but they are also full of the data required to work successfully with financial institutions.

I knew what I wanted to say, and LivePlan was user-friendly and had the perfect format for me to communicate precisely what bankers needed to know. Our business plan ended up being a huge success and helped us secure a six-figure loan in less than forty-five days.

However, I forgot something: in all of my planning, I neglected to write out what I wanted for myself. I assumed I could take on every aspect of the business without sleeping or eating regularly. This is not an exaggeration. I completely left myself out of the equation by putting myself into every role. I realized this about a year after opening the doors, and I started to share it with aspiring playground owners. This business was expensive to start and took many hours to run. I cut corners in my planning by assuming I could save in labor by taking on too many responsibilities.

As our business grew within the community and our online presence stretched to new areas of Louisiana, I started receiving calls from people who were ready to quit their jobs and start their own small businesses. I remember asking if anyone had a business plan, and not one person said yes. Why? Because business plan writing can be overwhelming. Even if you have a beautiful program to use, research is necessary before you get started. So I came up with twenty questions for business planning that I hoped would help. I knew that if I had been honest with myself and answered the last two of these questions, many scenarios could have played out differently.

I want you to be successful by learning what I missed. Here's the first step. If you want to open a business or revamp an existing one, ask yourself these questions:

<u>20 Business-Planning Questions</u>:
1. Why do you want to start your business? Do you have an origin story or concept?
2. What problem does your business solve?
3. How do you solve the problem?
4. Who is your ideal customer? Who do you plan to serve? Define your target market in terms of demographics (age, gender, income, etc.), geographics (neighborhood, climate, rural or urban, etc.), psychographics (interests, opinions, attitudes, etc.) and behavioral (habits).
5. Do you need a loan, or will you be financing the business yourself?
6. How much will it cost to start your business?
7. How much will it cost to run your business monthly?
8. How much cash do you have to cover costs until you are up and running?
9. Do you need a physical location? What type of facility do you require?

10. What capital purchases do you need to open this business?
11. Will you hire employees?
12. Do you require professional services for your start-up team? (lawyer, realtor, architect, banker, graphic designer, web designer, insurance agent, security company, contractor, etc.)
13. What will your business hours be? What days of the week will you offer your services?
14. What is the market like for your business?
15. Who is your competition?
16. What are the price points for your products? How much do they cost you to purchase or produce?
17. Is there a natural additional revenue stream you can add on easily to generate more sales?
18. How will you market your business? What companies can you partner with to cross-promote your businesses?
19. What will a day in the life of this company look like for you? Does this lifestyle meet your goals in all areas of your life?
20. If everything does not go as planned, do you still want to bring this product to market?

THE BUSINESS DIARIES

20 Questions

When starting my business, I mistook the instant success of the business plan without considering the life consequences. Questions 1–18 are as necessary as 19–20. Making modifications to my plan in the beginning, which we will discuss later, would have altered the trajectory of my life and business by avoiding circumstances that created burnout and financial risk.

If you are already running a business that doesn't look the way you planned, answer the above questions. A plan is a starting point and can change as your business grows and your clients provide feedback. Success comes from being able to reflect and course correct. Perhaps you will gain insight into a new strategy you can utilize to gain new traction, introduce an alternative offering, or even pivot completely.

What if the plan you write is too overwhelming? Then the best answer might be in the next section.

It's OK to Start Small

Sitting on my desk, tucked into the corner of a family photo from Maui, there's a fortune cookie message that reads, "All great things had small beginnings."

If the business planning questions made you feel overwhelmed, here is the advice I wish I had known: It is OK to start small.

When I was throwing my ideas together for an indoor party and playground venue, I thought I had to own the physical building for the events. That is absolutely not true. We created a 7,500-square-foot party place that cost half a million dollars to build out. I could have started small by throwing parties for people in their own homes or at parks with toys that targeted specific age groups and decor that was customized to our clients. Our main moneymaker was birthday parties. It's how we paid our bills. The walk-in play aspect of our business that was made popular by our giant play structure was a nice addition to the profits but wasn't completely necessary to start a profitable business. In my mind, I wanted a community where parents and caregivers could come together to watch their children enjoy the simplicity of playtime, but that could have technically been done anywhere.

When you start small, you can grow your business organically. You also learn what you like to offer clients and what doesn't work before you are committed to an investment that doesn't pay off in the long run. You can use profits to pay for capital improvements. Business growth can be done through word of mouth and on social media for free before investing advertising dollars that you may not have to spend.

Starting small might not seem as exciting, but it can be a great opportunity if you don't want to obtain a loan or go into debt with credit cards.

Looking at your business-planning questions from earlier in this chapter, is there a scaled-down version of a plan that would actually suit you better now? Would it allow you to begin sooner rather than later because you are not building out a physical space?

There is no shame in starting small. In fact, I would argue that there is no such thing as a small act. Every time we move forward in our business goals, we gain momentum.

The road we chose with our business was not small for us. I remember the day we found our location. It was a Honda motorcycle dealership that was built in 1972 and was well-known by many of our clients. The floors were cement and cold, the walls cinder block. Near the ceiling were two stripes, painted red and blue, that boasted "Honda." The brown walls were paneled to look like wood, and there was a lingering grease smell in the air that mixed with dirt that had been embedded in the floors for the last forty years. On one side was a rickety staircase made of metal that didn't go all the way to the wall and had huge gaps of space in between each tread. The second-floor mezzanine was visible from the first floor so the forklift could lift three-wheelers upstairs for storage. This wasn't quite the perfect space for an indoor playground, but the space itself worked. I could immediately see what might be if given the opportunity. But it takes a lot more than imagination to turn a motorcycle dealership into an indoor playground—it takes money. The decision to sign the lease on that building started the course of our experience. It took "small" off the table and introduced us to questions we hadn't answered in our business plan.

If you already have a business that feels large and overwhelming, it doesn't mean you can't start making small changes now to improve your situation, increase sales, and create the business you desire.

One thing can change everything. When we are in a panicked situation and try to change everything at once, it doesn't work. However, if you can focus on one change, that can course correct the future of your business.

In Secret Nine, we will talk more about the one thing that changed everything for me.

If you are embarking on a new enterprise and have a strong desire to open a physical location, how can you start small?

During COVID, I was so impressed by the businesses that pivoted. My favorite shops started to sell on Instagram and offered curbside pickups. Restaurants did the same. The entrepreneurs who complained didn't get anywhere, but the ones who didn't were everywhere. It was a huge lesson and one we can use post-pandemic.

Let's say, for example, you want to open a coffee shop. You have the latest version of healthy lattes, packed with nutrients, and your market is low on cafes. What are some smaller investments you can make? Perhaps a coffee cart on a popular corner? Could you deliver lattes to corporate offices? Could you go to farmers markets or piggyback on another restaurant that's already successful? There are endless options that can be done before you open the doors that might be more profitable than the original plan.

This topic of "smaller" allows you to grow bigger using money you have already made, which means less risk upfront. If I could change one thing during my entire experience, it would be to realize that starting small would have allowed me to grow big.

Secret Start-Up Steps for Today:

1. Start to answer your business planning questions 1–18.
2. Now answer questions 19–20. If you don't like the answer, where can you shift your potential plan to create the lifestyle you envision?
3. How can you start small? Is there a natural entry point that allows you to grow organically?

Take Action

Implement the Secret Start-Up Steps with the help of your free bonus bundle at heatherhays.co/book

A plan is a starting point and is allowed to change as your business grows and your clients provide feedback.

Secret Two

DON'T FUND YOUR LOAN TOO SOON

When asked for the truth regarding what went wrong in our business, I can answer that question with this chapter. My goal is that you will never be in a situation where your business dream becomes your entrepreneurial nightmare. Planning, researching, and preparing are not the same as implementing your business plan. If you are seeking a loan or building out a space, this chapter is for you.

After our business closed, one of my college friends kept asking me for specific numbers when I explained we had gone over budget. Once I provided the actual costs, she understood the severity of the situation much better. Therefore,

I am providing you with the same information. You can scale these numbers up or down depending on your situation. I just feel that offering transparency with the costs is the best way to share this information with you.

You Want Me to Wait to Fund My Loan?

Would you believe me if I told you that sometimes you want to wait on funding the loan you just worked so hard to obtain?

"Hey Heather, it's Chris from the bank. I have great news for you. My underwriter, who has worked here for eighteen years, loves your business plan."

My heart was beating with excitement. The banker continued, "Why don't you and Eric come in and sign some papers tomorrow, and we will get you set up with checks and a debit card and make this official."

I was beside myself. A bank had just consented to loaning me $200,000 to start my dream of owning my own business. After we signed all the paperwork to fund our loan, our banker said, "Congratulations, Mrs. and Mr. Hays. We can't wait for opening day." We shook hands with Chris and drove home excited about all the possibilities.

The loan was set up to be amortized over five years. We originally believed we could use some of our start-up money to pay off the loan faster once we were ready for opening day. Reality could not have been farther from the truth. The loan lasted all sixty of those long months. The automatic debit took place on the 5th of every month, and on the night of the 4th, I would ensure there were ample funds to cover the payment.

The $200,000 dwindled so quickly that two months after we obtained the loan, we were already drawing from our savings account we had planned on using later in the year. By October we were taking loans from our investment accounts. And by December we were utilizing Eric's paychecks from the set to ensure we covered vendor payments on time.

So what went wrong? In three words, the build-out.

For a specialized business, you have to have the right building. When you have a limited budget, you aren't going to build something; you are going to build out an existing facility.

I would argue that who you sign the lease with as your landlord is almost as important as the location. I had to look for a very specific location with certain attributes to make my business work. For instance, this would be an event-led business, which meant I needed parking. I also had to find a central location that wasn't too far from a neighborhood that could afford my type of business. Moms are notorious multi-taskers, so I really liked the idea of being close to grocery stores and the mall so parents could hit a quick errand and then reward their children with some fun playtime. I wanted my business to feel like a destination and party spot but also be a building you might pass for a hundred other reasons that would catch your eye for the future.

We looked at over forty real estate lease listings. The building we chose already had air conditioning and space for a large parking lot and was owned by a family who had built the building in the 1970s and knew the ins and outs of it intimately. This was a huge plus because they had a built-in crew of professionals who had worked on it over the years that we could tap if something happened.

It also allowed us to have a relationship with the owners because they cared about their building. The landlord's father had built it and since passed away, and to her, a children's destination was a fun way to use the facility. I remember her giggling with just the idea of it when we first met with her for the walk-through. We were also fortunate that her daughter was similar to my age and was the broker running her real estate rentals. Julie was a savvy business leader in her industry and constantly offered good advice. She was someone who knew how to get things done efficiently and successfully.

When we found our spot on the service road with amazing landlords, I thought our long, hard search was over. You can dream up the perfect business plan, but until you actually sign the lease, you truly have no idea what you are getting into. The lease will determine your start-up costs in many ways because of the build-out.

At this point, little did I know that a specialized business meant specialized zoning laws. I assumed going to the city planner's office would help me determine the best way to move forward with the project. But that was not true. They explained that I had to have a "design professional" walk me through the rules. In other words, I needed to hire an architect to design the plans and then take them to the city for approval. This is where our problems began. The answer to our problem begins with this question, which action step should we take first: fund the loan, sign the lease or get city approval for the build out?

What Went Wrong

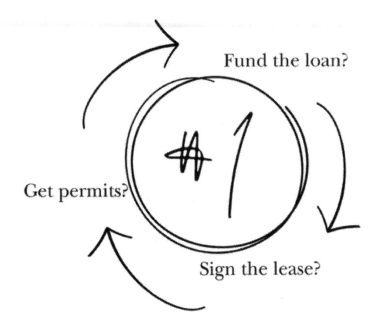

Here is a rundown of what went wrong:

- The construction timeline took much longer than expected. We signed the lease the first week of July 2012. We had the following grand opening dates planned: August 1, September 15, and October 1 and advertised accordingly. We finally opened December 1, 2012.
- Our plans were not approved by the Parish (Louisiana's name for cities) several times due to noncompliance with zoning codes. Fortunately we had a patient architect and

contractor who were both experienced and kind. They went to bat for us on numerous occasions, writing letters and appearing at hearings.
- Permitting takes a long time if you are changing the usage of a building. We worked with the Parish from late April until early July to determine if we could move forward with just signing the lease. Remember, our loan was funded in June, so we were already paying down the initial $200,000 loan. We filed for our permit in late July and did not receive the permit to work until October 12, five and a half months after beginning our work with the architect and contractor.
- Our build-out was more expensive than planned. Our final start-up costs went from $280,000 to $410,000. Some of the extra expenses included the following:
  - New stairs: $18,630
  - New parking lot: $26,962
  - Striping for parking lot: $1,633
  - Glass storefront: $6,890
  - Additional electric: $16,834

The cycle of fear and lack started at this point. Before we ever opened, my husband and I would say, "Palm Tree Playground is going to have to pay for itself." The reason we said that was because we had now used all of our first-year reserves on the build-out.

What Could Have Gone Right

So what would an alternative scenario have looked like for us? How could we have prevented this spiral from happening? The following are some of the things we could have done:

- Talked to our banker or financial planner about options for waiting on funding the loan until we were ready.
- Since our building's usage was being converted—had the approved permit in hand before finalizing the lease.
- Paid our architect to accompany us to the permitting department to ensure the correct questions were asked to provide the correct answers.
- Negotiated large building improvements with the landlord even though we were signing a triple net lease.
- Waited to ship large items until the build-out was complete so we didn't have to store them offsite.

Further, we interviewed multiple architects and contractors, and their pricing was vastly different. What we learned was, until you get the plans in front of the permit department, none of it is accurate anyway. The smart choice would have been to spend money up front that we were willing to walk away from if the plan didn't get passed before we signed the lease. We didn't do that because we didn't want to "waste" money. Instead of being proactive, we created a reactive situation based on the decisions of the parish planners. The mind set became, "This is happening to us," instead of feeling confident that we were "making things happen" in a positive way for the business.

If you are building out a space or changing a building's usage, employ your design professional to go to the city for you to get permits and obtain answers.

Make sure you and your contractor have a detailed timeline and budget you both sign off on. Have them understand that barring any catastrophe or natural disaster, this timeline will cost you money, and therefore if they don't deliver, it will cost them money as well.

It is easy to see all of these solutions now, but in the moment, they were not apparent. Experience is a fantastic teacher if you can see the lessons once you process the mistakes. This is the most important information I know to share if you are obtaining a loan or building out a space. Remember, a small amount of money invested up front can save you from wasting a large amount later.

Secret Start-Up Steps for Today:

1. Create a start-up timeline for either your new business or a new project in your existing business.
2. Determine if you will have to make a small investment upfront to ensure your large investment pays off in your allotted time frame.
3. Schedule a meeting with your investor or banker about how you can maximize the capital you have.

Take Action

Implement the Secret Start-Up Steps with the help of your free bonus bundle at heatherhays.co/book

Experience is a fantastic teacher if you can see the lessons once you process the mistakes.

Secret Three

YOU ARE NOT ALONE: CREATE A TEAM, USE THE APP, AND IDENTIFY YOUR POWER PLAYERS

I felt so alone. I was in a new city with a new business plan and two little girls. I wanted to build Palm Tree Playground (PTP) more than anything. Our morning routine was to go to the gym, and while I worked out, Madison and McKenzie played in the kids club. They loved it, and a big part of that joy was the young woman who ran it named Erin. She was smart, organized, extremely friendly, and just the type of person I would love to have opening PTP with me. Luckily, she was up for a challenge. We worked side by side for months ordering equipment, decorating the facility, researching systems, and interviewing team members. It takes one person, and suddenly you are no longer alone. Your ideas exponentially expand when you have the right person to bounce them off of and receive feedback from. It's amazing what the power of support can bring into an entrepreneur's life, because a start-up business can feel lonely. Unless your friends and family have gone through this process before, it's hard to share the demands you are facing while opening and then running your small business.

From this experience, I have three solutions for not feeling alone that were invaluable to me. These three solutions include creating a team, using available technology to run your business, and identifying professional power players who can assist you with important decisions. Let's go through them one by one now.

Create a Team NOW

Palm Tree Playground might have been a cash-poor business, but we were rich with employees. We struck gold many times with amazing people who joined our company. I truly believe the individuals who work for you should be viewed as valuable team members and each person brings something special to the business. When we were spending cash quickly, I had a fear of spending money on payroll. However, to run an indoor playground successfully, I had to have ample staff to oversee the operations. This is true of many small businesses, including restaurants and retail establishments.

Clients asked me all the time how I had such an amazing staff, and I would joke that all I needed to start my hiring process was "Erin and the triplets." That's because our first manager, Erin, referenced above, who was both hardworking and incredibly smart, had a cousin who was dating a triplet. "The triplets," also known as Alicia, Allie, and Alyssa, were also amazing individuals, and PTP went from no team members to four overnight. Like many small businesses, we did not require specific training to qualify for employment status, such as a bachelor's degree or specific certification program, so there was no feeder school or program to target to hire the right people. Therefore, our process for finding talented team members was not organized at first. As opening day came faster and faster, Erin and I realized we had to hire team members *now*, so we came up with the following strategy.

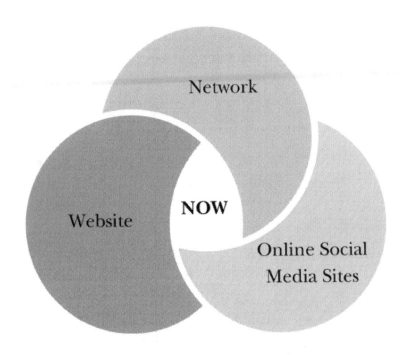

NOW Hiring Strategy Methods:

- Networking
- Online Social Media Sites
- Website

Networking for jobs is important at every level in most industries. It turns out it was absolutely necessary for a business that survived on good reviews and happy parents. Our network hiring process was very simple. It started with Erin and the triplets. We had so many team members we valued that we interviewed their friends and family to work with us too. Most times the referral was successful. In fact, we had so many students from one particular high school working with us that every year upon graduation, we would ask for five new up-and-coming seniors who could replace the graduates who'd just left for college. Clients would constantly ask for our party hosts' names and numbers for babysitting jobs, and we did lose a few to nanny positions. Although we were sad, it was a huge compliment to our business.

Online social media sites have grown exponentially since we opened in 2012. But even then, we had success just by posting our upcoming job positions before we even opened. Word of mouth about a new indoor playground spread quickly, and our social media pages started picking up a small following. Once we began posting job positions, potential clients realized that we were indeed opening soon. It was actually a wonderful way to spread the word that we were not only hiring but also we were preparing for our grand opening and to stay tuned! It also gave us something else to post about on our social media pages. The "Coming Soon" messages were stale after five months, and the "Apply Now" messages got a lot more interaction even though most people were not looking for jobs.

Our last method for hiring was our company website. This is obvious, I know. It was so simple, but it actually drove potential clients to our webpage because they followed the link from social media even though they had no interest in applying for a job. We had a built-in form on the page that allowed people to apply directly, and it was incredibly easy to follow up from there.

Use the App!

Sometimes apps are so perfectly designed and user-friendly that you feel they were created just for you. After trial and error, we found some apps that literally saved us from making mistakes that were both costly and embarrassing. When we first opened Palm Tree Playground, I tried to save money by using spreadsheets for everything. I either didn't have the time to research a better solution or didn't think I could afford it. A few years into running PTP, however, I realized every time I needed something specific to run the business, there was an app for that. Yes, it cost money, but it was absolutely worth it.

Here are a few case studies from Palm Tree Playground.

<u>Party Center Software:</u>

Imagine opening a worksheet on your computer where you keep your party scheduling document and realizing that you have double-booked a party. In 2013, the January and February dates lined up exactly, and we had booked a party for January 15, 2013, that was supposed to be on February 15, 2023. The only problem was, we already had another party booked for February 15. It was a difficult situation because the invitations had gone out and we needed to offer the party mom a solution. Fortunately, we were able to move one of the parties and offer a heavy discount to the accommodating party. However, I knew we could not continue down this path as we continued to grow.

We made most of our revenue through birthday parties. Our facility could host up to fifteen parties a weekend, so over the course of a month, that was sixty parties. Each party needed a room choice, theme option, pizza option, party host, contact person, guest of honor, and deposit. I was using a spreadsheet with no sharing options for my managers. If I was out of the office, I would have to call my managers with date options to book a party. I literally thought to myself, "It would be so nice if someone invented software to make this easier." Then, at the height of my spreadsheet stress due to the double booking, I found Party Centre Software. It was literally designed for event venues identical to mine. The software was intuitive for what I needed to run my parties efficiently because the inventor was an owner/operator like me. With it, I was no longer the only person who could book parties, and online bookings were now an option.

We could record deposits, schedule parties, send receipts and confirmation emails, and even choose all the food options at the bookings! It saved hours of time and allowed us to book parties online when no one was working at the facility outside of normal business hours. It also prevented potential mistakes of double bookings. This one program completely changed how we did business, and it made me want to find other ways to save time and energy.

WhenIWork.Com:

Another spreadsheet we used was for scheduling our team members. It was laborious and tedious to plan out when every single person would work for two weeks in advance and then receive everyone's comments about how the schedule did not accommodate their schedule. It took hours. Then we realized there was an app for that!

Instead of emailing our team a bi-weekly schedule, I now had an app that everyone could download to their phones. Everyone was labeled as either a manager or party host in the system. The team member would block out dates they were unable to work, and that way the manager couldn't assign them to the day. Genius! It was so simple yet worked so well. No more emails back and forth about finals, vacations, or prom dates. They would just put in their requested time off, and it was no longer an issue.

Managers could look at the party schedule for the upcoming weekend and add shifts as necessary. Anyone could grab them. Dropped shifts were immediately picked up by someone wanting more hours. Because we knew who was available and who was not, we were no longer over-scheduling party hosts in case they couldn't make it. This saved us money in payroll costs.

The team members appreciated the ease of use and the fact they were now in control of their schedule. I loved it because I was saving hours each week and money in payroll. It was a win-win situation.

This app can be used for any business. If you employ more than four people on your team who don't have a set schedule, this is a fantastic app to start with to utilize your time more efficiently.

LivePlan.Com

I mentioned LivePlan in the first secret about business plan writing. This website was essential in taking our knowledge about the playground industry and writing up a succinct plan to obtain a loan. The website is not offered as an app but was so instrumental to our foundation that I wanted to include it. Software can make your product look professional, and this is one example of that. I knew all the information I needed to convey, but I wasn't sure how to put it into the proper format to submit to an underwriter. I clearly remember sitting at my computer with pages of notes, bank statements, and research, wondering what to do with it all. LivePlan offered that assistance.

It has been twelve years since I wrote that business plan, and LivePlan has grown in that time and offers even more options for small business solutions, including advisors and mentors. This company's product contributed greatly to our initial success, and I urge any entrepreneur to research how LivePlan might help them too.

Identify Your Power Players

Power players offer professional services that maximize your business potential to build a foundation for success. They help optimize profits and assess risk to keep you moving forward. Power players are a separate category from the vendors we partner with, which will be covered in Secret 6. Not every business will need all of these professional services. However, it's great to have recommendations on hand in case you need them.

For example, we never planned on using a land surveyor, but when the parish required more parking for compliance, we needed to hire one to ascertain how much land we could use. Our security specialist was also not budgeted. However, when zoning mandated that we install fire sprinklers that were cost prohibitive, we were able to instead install an elaborate fire alarm system.

Here is a list of power players you may need for your business:

- Accountant
- Ad agency brand manager
- Architect
- Attorney
- Banker
- Contractor
- Graphic designer
- Insurance broker
- Land surveyor
- Payroll specialist (payroll and HR)
- Security specialist
- Real estate broker

Professional power players can be as involved as you want according to your budget and needs. Our attorney gave me the best advice early on in our journey when the build-out was over budget and we were facing another set of delays with construction. I asked her how entrepreneurs protect themselves from these scenarios. She stated simply, "Sometimes they can't. There is risk in business, and you have to decide if it's worth working toward your goal." She was right, of course. I couldn't predict every scenario that would happen, but instead, I had to move forward with the best intentions and make good business decisions. Having professional power players in place helped me make those decisions and can help you do the same.

Secret Start-Up Steps for Today:

1. Create a team: What team members support you? If you are a solopreneur, is there a consultant you can hire for your busy times?
2. Use the app: Explore apps that can ease your workload. What one app will you research this week?
3. Power players: Make a list of your power players with contact information. Remember, you are not alone!

Take Action

Implement the Secret Start-Up Steps with the help of your free bonus bundle at heatherhays.co/book

We might have been cash poor but we were rich with employees.

Secret Four

POPULARITY DOESN'T ALWAYS EQUAL PROFITABILITY

It was the Friday afternoon at the beginning of Christmas vacation, and I looked around the packed playground to where my friend was grinning at me ear to ear, making a motion with her hands like she was collecting something in the air. She then mouthed, "You are raking in the money!"

There were so many kids, nine and under, climbing all over the play structure. The toddler area was full. Parents were packed into the cafe area, laughing and relaxing into their upcoming holiday vacation.

I thought to myself that I could see why she thought we are successful. It looked like we were super popular, and that day, we were. What my friend didn't know, however, was that all of this popularity was not being translated into profit. We were building brand awareness, but it was not converting into sales, and popularity doesn't always keep you profitable.

Brand Awareness

In today's society of followers and likes, it is easy to get lost in the idea that your business's popularity equates to your prosperity. However, it's not that simple, as there are plenty of "popular" businesses that fail and a number of businesses you have never heard of that thrive.

The *Oxford Dictionary* says *popularity* is "the state or condition of being liked, admired, or supported by many people."

In many instances of social media, we look to be *liked* and *admired* but fail to be *supported*.

Brand awareness, according to *Forbes*, "is the level of recognition and familiarity that a brand has among its target audience."

And there was the problem at Palm Tree Playground. Your target audience needs to be familiar with your brand, but what if you are spending your time and energy on the wrong segment of your audience and with the wrong message?

We had spent two years building a brand that centered on an indoor playground that hosted parties and playdates, where the message should have been an indoor party venue that offers a playground. We knew that the majority of our income was derived from parties, but for a long time we concentrated on creating a brand without a solid message or offer.

It is essential that your brand reaches your target market with a valuable message and offers the solution to your ideal customer's problem or pain point. If your marketing message doesn't drive traffic to the place where you make sales, then it's not successful, and your popularity won't translate into sales.

How do you turn your popularity into profits? Your brand messaging, marketing, and advertising have to lead back to your website, and on your website, you have to have an offer. An offer is how you make money and what the marketing message directly points to.

Make an Offer

What makes a good offer?

- The offer addresses a problem and offers a solution for your target market.
- The offer is super clear.
- The offer is of high value to your target market.

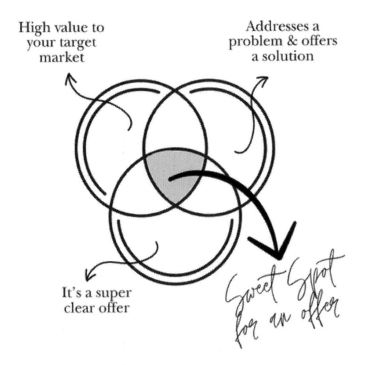

This is why knowing your target market is so important. Who are you selling to? In our case, we had five different types of clients we wanted to attract, but at the end of the day, only one made us money, and we had to start creating a message about birthday party services to attract them. If you look back at your business-planning questions, you answered who your ideal target market is. Are you creating offers that are attractive to that group? Does your messaging convey a valuable offer to your target market that will grow your business?

One mistake businesses can make is creating a lot of unclear messaging. People knowing about your business is different from them knowing what you do. If you don't tell them how you can be valuable to them, who will? If you don't offer them something to buy, how will they know what you sell?

In your mind you might think you are being specific, but does a potential client know the following:

- Who your business serves
- What products your business offers
- How your products are valuable to them

Once you know your target market, you ensure your messaging speaks to that group and the offer is valuable to them.

Metrics and Key Performance Indicators

How do you know if your offering is working? This is where you use metrics. *Metrics* are quantifiable measurements to track the performance of a specific business function. There are a number of metric categories businesses use to determine success: sales, marketing, customer service, and employee experience are some examples. Creating a set of metrics that allow you to track growth requires you to decide what you want to accomplish in your business and ensure the marketing message supports that.

Let's use an example of an email list since we know it is an essential growth tool for small businesses. When you build a list, you own that list, and it cannot be taken away like a social media account. Additionally, email lists are very specialized to what you do, giving you a captive audience. Emails build rapport with great content and share offerings that lead to higher sales revenue.

Now that you understand why email lists are so important, let's say your first goal is to build a list of five thousand email addresses. Let's look at some simple metrics you can utilize to track your success and determine if the list is earning you the desired sales outcome.

Five Metrics to Track Weekly:
1. List growth rate
2. Open rate
3. Clickthrough rate
4. Conversion rate
5. Return on investment

List growth rate: The rate at which your email list grows.

Formula:

New Subscribers - Unsubscribers/Total Email Addresses × 100

Open rate: How many email recipients open the email.

Formula:

Number of Opened Emails/Number of Delivered Emails × 100

Clickthrough rate: The number of readers who click through to your website from a link contained in your email.

Formula:

Clicks/Delivered Emails × 100

Conversion rate: The number of readers who completed your goal once they clicked through to your website.

Formula:

Goal Completion/Delivered Emails × 100

Return on investment: The return on investment of your email campaign.

Formula:

$ Additional Sales - $ Investment in Email Campaign/$ Investment in Email Campaign × 100

Many businesses pay large amounts of marketing dollars that outweigh the sales they earn from the messaging. These businesses might appear to be very successful because they are everywhere, when in fact their advertising budget is cutting into their profits. It's a calculated move to spend more in advertising than you earn in sales. Some businesses do this successfully and the sales eventually outweigh the advertising dollars spent, but it's not sustainable for all business models.

Your competition might be doing this and you would never know. This reality struck me when I decided to sell my business and met with other owners in the area who shared the same type of clients. I was offering to sell our high-end equipment at a remarkable deal, but no one else could make the investment because of similar cash flow issues. They had created the illusion of success as I had because people want to do business with successful people.

The good news is, if you already have a large following or name in the community, you can use that to increase sales by redirecting your messaging and offers that focus on driving up sales. If you do not have a name yet, you can use this information to plan growth for your brand awareness.

Secret Start-Up Steps for Today:

Answer the following questions:

1. How is your business liked, admired, and supported by your current level of brand awareness?
2. What is your current messaging?
3. What offer does your marketing support?
4. What metrics will you start tracking today?

Take Action

Implement the Secret Start-Up Steps with the help of your free bonus bundle at heatherhays.co/book

In many instances of social media, we look to be liked and admired but fail to be supported.

Secret Five

MAKE SALESPEOPLE YOUR BUSINESS PARTNERS

Salespeople Can Add or Take Away from Your Business

I believe salespeople can be one of your greatest advocates in your small business, but they have to understand what you are selling and what you value. On the flip side of that, you have to know what you are really selling and what you really value as well.

One afternoon I left the playground and was picking up my daughters at a friend's house when my manager called in a panic. She'd just had the most unusual run-in with one of the customers who had purchased a discount ticket to our business online. In an effort to grow our customer base, we'd participated in a discount walk-in play coupon. I'd heard great reviews about this promotional company, and although I wasn't really looking to build up the walk-in play business, I felt desperate and would try anything to build awareness around our brand.

Our manager went on to explain that an irate grandmother had just left the facility because a two-year-old came up to her in the toddler area and hit her in the face. I was confused, to say the least. Grandparents were some of our biggest fans, and I did not understand how it was our fault that the toddler hit this woman. The answer is, the grandmother was upset that the child's mother did not reprimand that child and thought that we should step in to say something. She went on to report our business to the Better Business Bureau, and although this might sound laughable, it took a lot of time and energy to deal with in the long run. This event happened because I focused on building the wrong part of the business. Walk-in play sales did not produce the income I needed and the circumstance could have been avoided altogether if I had stuck to my party business building goals.

A few months later we had another opportunity to promote our business: "This beautiful magazine featuring your ad will increase your revenue by targeting high-end neighborhoods that don't currently know your business exists."

It sounded amazing, and I definitely wanted to introduce PTP to those zip codes. The magazine was well done, but there was a catch: I had to offer a "gift" with the ad. We chose to offer a $50 coupon to anyone who booked a party with us in this new demographic. We searched our database and knew that very few of our current clients lived in the areas of the city these coupons would go to. The ad created some new business, but then something happened that I didn't expect. Well-meaning friends and family members who received the magazine clipped the coupons and gave them to parents who had already booked their parties with us. For every new party we booked, five parties already existed, which canceled out the money from the new party. Of course, certain language was included in the ad that would have prevented people from using the coupon, but in those cases, some people went so far as to cancel their party and rebook with the coupon, so we chose to honor it regardless of the circumstance out of good faith. When I canceled the advertising agreement, the sales rep was legitimately shocked that the product had backfired.

Both of these stories taught me a valuable lesson about how to work with salespeople. I needed them to partner with me so that both of our successes were tied together. The above scenarios didn't have a huge downside to the rep, but the stakes were higher for us. We couldn't afford to waste time worrying about toddlers' antics or waste money discounting parties we had already sold. I was constantly discounting my high-end product, which literally cheapened it.

It is easy to be overwhelmed by all of the new salespeople who enter your life once you cut that ribbon on opening day. I was constantly called downstairs to our lobby to be introduced to someone who had a new product or promotion that Palm Tree Playground just couldn't run without.

At first, I was enthusiastic about the new products and tried many of them optimistically. Then I turned weary because our money was low and I felt guilty turning well-meaning salespeople away. Eventually, I felt like we were being taken advantage of and every new salesperson through the door, on the phone, or in an email was a potential threat. I needed to look at this differently to succeed, but I had so many examples of what didn't work. I wanted to get out of the space of being over-promised and underserved. That's why I came up with my Sales Empowerment List.

Sales Empowerment List

I created the following Sales Empowerment List for myself to elevate the products and promotions I partnered with. You can use it in your business to do the same:

- You are a specialist in your community and the authority for your product. You know your business better than anyone else.
- Successful vendors enhance your business, not detract from it. It's safe to be supported by them.
- You choose who you do and do not work with, and there is no guilt required in saying, "No thank you."
- Not all marketing products promote your business in the right way. You don't have to do everything.

- If a product or promotion doesn't serve your ideal client, don't offer, sell or promote it.

Further, it's necessary to line up future promotions with your future plans.

A good set of questions to ask yourself is as follows:

- Does this promotion add value to my existing clientele?
- Does my ideal client need this product or promotion?
- Why am I considering offering this promotion? How does this plan help me reach my goals?
- What guarantees is this company offering?
- Does this company do business in a way that I want to partner with them?

Synergistically, all of these facets should work together to benefit both your business and their company. I think there is magic in finding "partners." You can either fear salespeople or embrace them. Just remember, if their products solve one of your pain points, they might make a good partner for you. Well-intentioned salespeople can have great ideas for how you can improve your business, but at the end of the day, they truly don't know what is going on behind the scenes unless they ask the right questions and you are open to sharing with them. Don't get bogged down by the trap of the "next best thing." Everyone is selling the best item in their category according to them. Remember, we need little improvements that make huge impacts, not huge investments that make little impact.

If you are a people pleaser, it might be difficult to say no to products and services at times. To be honest, it can feel humiliating if the reason is that you can't afford what they are offering. This comes from a place of lack, and bad business decisions are made if desperation is the overwhelming feeling. Instead, consider being open to the possibility of working with someone fantastic when the timing is correct.

Sales Partnership Questionnaire

To plan for potential partnerships with salespeople, you can create a simple Sales Partnership Questionnaire for when you receive an email or onsite visitor.

It can be something as simple as the following:

> Hi, my name is Heather. I'm the owner of Palm Tree Playground, and I partner with companies who help me grow my business. Please feel free to answer the questions below if you would like to meet.

- What product do you offer?
- Is there another company in the immediate area you work with?
- How can I find you online to learn more?

Once they reply, read the responses and decide if you can meet with them. There's nothing wrong with someone knocking on your door to offer a product. It's helpful in many cases. But time is limited in an entrepreneur's day, and if you haven't scheduled time out for sales calls, you might not get other relevant work accomplished.

If you choose to set up a meeting, consider the Sales Meeting List:

- Remember your Sales Empowerment List.
- View salespeople as potential business partners. If they don't treat you as an equal with a genuine interest in your business, move on.
- Negotiate with salespeople if you are interested in a certain product. They might not say yes, but it's nice to know what's possible.
- Do not be guilted into making a purchase.
- Ask them how they can partner with you. An easy way to do this is, "I understand this product costs $X per month. How can we partner together to make it work best for

your sales numbers and for mine?" They both need to go up together, or it's not a product that will work for either company. Let them know that you are looking for someone to work with long-term and not for a quick fix, because those don't truly exist in your industry.
- Ask them what they know about your industry and if they have any personal affiliation with it.

Once I adapted this mindset in regard to salespeople, we experienced growth in ways we could have never planned. In the following sections, I share a few of these success stories.

Success Stories:

Party City

One day I was called down to the lobby, where there was a salesperson from Party City. First, I didn't know that there were actual salespeople from Party City that would come and check on accounts like mine. Second, I was completely turned off at first because I thought he was going to sell to me, but instead he was so kind and genuinely interested in our facility and asked to see the different party rooms. I was happy to give the tour and show him the upstairs three party rooms. He was quiet for a minute, and then he said to me, "You know, I call on a facility that's a little bit like this in Mississippi, and they have one room that's completely designated for a certain popular party theme." Intrigued, I asked him to elaborate, and he explained the owners had purchased all of the decorations for a specific themed party, and business grew exponentially because it took the stress off the parents to decorate.

It just so happened that a very popular movie had just been released featuring an ice queen. Party parents were always bringing in blue tulle and snowflakes to try to decorate for the favored theme. So our managers and I sat down and brainstormed. How could we create a beautiful party room that was themed? One of our rooms was already painted light blue, so we designed simple centerpieces with icicles and snowflakes. We hung snowflakes from the ceiling and purchased a wintry backdrop. When the room was complete, we advertised it in the popular New Orleans family magazine.

Very quickly, we sold out of Ice Queen parties. It was such a great idea that we ended up designing many other party rooms, including space wars, the mouse room, surfer dude, rainbow, and super hero. Not only was it great for parents because it took the stress of decorating off of them, but also it made us income we needed.

The sales rep ensured he offered all the supplies we needed to run all of those rooms. He really became a business partner of mine in the sense that he cared about my success, which also helped his success. In good business deals, everyone can come away as a winner.

Tork

George was another favorite vendor at Palm Tree Playground. He sold paper and soap supplies for a company called Tork. Although this is not as exciting as decorated party rooms, George kept our important supplies stocked, and Tork provided all the commercial-grade dispensers that instantly elevated the space into looking professional. This was not something I thought about during the build-out phase. George's attention to detail took something off my plate that I didn't even know I needed. He made owning a business so much easier and with a gracious attitude.

Media Partners

Media partners like *Nola Family Magazine*, New Orleans Mom's Blog, and *Saint Charles Magazine* designed beautiful features and festive events to increase our revenue by introducing us to new readership, providing us value through out-of-the-box thinking.

We received a huge bump in business from these relationships, just to name a few, and many partnerships developed with fellow entrepreneurs who valued growing their product along with ours.

The great news is, you can use this strategy starting today. Make a list of compatible businesses to yours that you can partner with but are not considered competition. See how you can benefit each other and grow sales as a result. By working together you can reach and serve more people.

Secret Start-Up Steps for Today:

1. Make a list of your current vendors.
2. Highlight the names of the vendors you see as business partners.
3. Schedule a meeting with one of those vendors to discuss future growth opportunities.

Take Action

Implement the Secret Start-Up Steps with the help of your free bonus bundle at heatherhays.co/book

Successful sales people enhance your business not detract from it.

Secret Six

BAD CLIENTS TEACH AND GOOD CLIENTS PREACH

The Bad Client

It was opening day, and I was staring at my first bad client while she mocked my business that was three hours old. I could see the angry, disappointed expressions on her face.

There was a comparison happening. She was looking at her phone and then glancing around the facility—the facility that I had just sunk all of my money into, the business that would cost me in ways I could never imagine over the next five years. She was belittling something in thirty-nine seconds that I had contemplated for years—the time it took to save the money, write the plan, and survive the build-out. But I don't mean just that; I mean the dream of owning a business.

She was disapproving of me like a stern mother to her disobedient child. I was drawn to her because my defenses were up. I was ready for a fight. I was ready to express that what I'd done and how I had done it were only with good intentions.

I walked up to her and introduced myself. There was an expression on her face between snotty indignance and feigned regret of spending $6.50 on the entrance fee.

"I am just not seeing all the things listed on your website." She shook her head like an exhausted, overwhelmed schoolteacher. "Y'all say that a company called Soft Play designed your equipment, but it is hard and hurting my child's knees. There is nothing on the walls. The cafe area doesn't have much food—" she cut off in exasperation.

I didn't defend myself. I found myself agreeing with her. "Well, I am sorry you feel that way. We were over budget due to build-out costs, and I couldn't afford the mural. The food is coming, and our play equipment is the best in the industry. Let me get something real quick."

I ran up a flight of stairs and grabbed my start-up notebook with the beautiful mural in it. I found the dubious woman and said, "This is the mural we couldn't afford. Isn't it cute? Kids playing at the beach." I looked at it wistfully because my desire for that mural was strong and my not understanding the full build-out process had blocked me from this focal detail.

Then I saw it rush across her face: embarrassment. Not enough to apologize, of course. Just a little reality that I was a mom doing my absolute best to create something, and in five minutes she had torn it apart. Every part of it.

Why did her opinion matter so much to me? Because we live in a review-and-post society, so the reviews have to mean something, right? Was I missing the bigger picture here? Would I let her destroy the happiness of my opening day?

I took back my power in that moment and walked away. I said my piece, and that was how it would have to stand.

Six months later, I was checking parents in at the front cash register, and she walked in briefly, catching my eye before quickly looking away. I held my head high. She was back, so her child must have liked his previous experience. Plus, her opinion was only allowed to bother me once. I was not engaging in round two with her. Finally, we had hit the six-month mark and all the little quirks were worked out. We had bright, beachy décor and a full snack stand, and our business was busy.

Palm Tree Playground had evolved, had she?

It was her turn to pay, and I welcomed her with a smile that hopefully didn't have a smirk hidden in it. She spilled immediately, "I am so sorry for how I behaved. I have been here a few times since the opening day, and your staff is wonderful, the play equipment is always clean, and my son really loves it."

I accepted her apology and moved forward. However, the interaction taught me a lot. I realized my insecurities allowed me to agree with her criticism as soon as the first complaint left her mouth. All of my good intentions for running a business that improved the community were immediately forgotten, and instead I listened to her opinion of what we had created. Here is what I learned:

- Remember your intentions for starting and running your business. Do not let one negative comment derail that effort.
- If there is a constructive idea you can learn, use it. If not, move on.
- Not everyone has to like what you create, and perhaps that person is not your ideal client.

- Do not allow other people's bad attitudes affect your good one.
- Your ideal client will respond to what you have created and your messaging. Focus on that.

The Good Client

I can think of one hundred good clients right now and at least twenty more exceptional ones. We had party moms give us huge hugs at the end of their celebrations, grandparents write letters to thank us, and caregivers spend hours with us while the children played. I have hundreds of birthday party photos from those five years of smiling faces and grateful hearts. These clients made everything we did more special and inspired us to do more. They enjoyed what we offered and respected the rules and parameters in which we did it.

Like attracts like, and I think our positive team members, happy environment, and high-end offerings invited many wonderful people into our facility. Here are some truths about good clients:

- Good customers spread the word for you in a way advertising never can: the customer experience through positive reviews.

- Good customers bring their friends to your business and are repeat customers.
- Good customers create a great atmosphere for your team and make their work experience better.
- Good customers introduce you to potential business partnerships and growth opportunities in the community.
- Good customers offer valuable feedback to help you grow your business.

How to Show Client Appreciation

Good clients are those you nurture relationships with. Make the good clients top of mind instead of the negative clients. Serve them well. There are simple ways to thank clients that are either free or affordable that go a long way to demonstrate you value them. You don't have to have a huge budget. Maybe you don't have any budget at all! That's OK, we are looking for simple ways to offer gratitude. You can consistently grow your appreciation over the years, and what starts small can flourish later.

We thanked every party family with a free play pass to return in the future and opened our doors early for customers who had membership passes.

Here are some simple ways you can show your clients appreciation:

- Write thank-you notes or social media messages.
- Respond to your clients' reviews with a thank-you of your own.
- Offer special hours for repeat customers.
- Provide "insider" knowledge of an upcoming sale or promotion by using your email list.
- Learn your clients' names and use them.
- Create a complimentary coffee or water station.
- Tell your clients how much you appreciate their feedback and how you used it to improve a product or process.
- Send a holiday message.

- Start a monthly giveaway that you can run on social media.
- Be consistent with whatever client appreciation choice you make, and let it become something everyone looks forward to on a regular basis.

Secret Start-Up Steps for Today:

1. Answer the following: What can you learn from a negative client that can have a positive impact instead of a negative one?
2. Create a list of ten clients you value.
3. Come up with a way to show your appreciation to these ten clients. Consider a simple email or note to thank them for their loyalty.

Take Action

Implement the Secret Start-Up Steps with the help of your free bonus bundle at heatherhays.co/book

Remember your intentions for starting and running your business. Do not let one negative comment derail that effort.

Secret Seven
VOLUNTEER WITH PURPOSE

Lack of Success Substitution

When you volunteer intentionally, you change the world, but when you volunteer for everything in order to fill a void, you can destroy your own world.

My lack of success in business created this drive to volunteer because at least I could be successful at that. If I were working for free, I wouldn't be scared to ask people for donations, money, or time.

In New Orleans, there is always a party, and generous donors line up for a good cause. I would say yes to almost anything offered to me in a volunteer capacity because it made me feel good to help people. This meant I ran both my girls' scout troops, co-chaired the school fair four years in a row, chaired various Junior League committees, co-chaired the table decorations committee for the annual Children's Hospital gala, and even joined the board of the local cancer organization. I loved all of it, and it was meaningful, but it also caused large amounts of stress because I did all of this important work simultaneously.

After I went through a particularly stressful season, I knew I'd hit rock bottom and had to change my volunteer efforts.

I decided I wanted to use my natural talents for leadership and combine them with my passion, which was female entrepreneurship. The Junior League was launching a new committee to sponsor a pitch contest at New Orleans Entrepreneur Week, and I knew I had to be part of it. Fortunately, I was chosen for the committee co-chair position, and soon the hard work began to find contestants and create a formidable event.

Through the Goldman Sachs 10KSB program that I completed the year before, I was able to introduce our contestants to a fabulous coach who was willing to prep them for the event for free. It is a partnership that continues today as of 2023 when I'm writing this. We had a popular New Orleans business owner emcee the event and three successful businesswomen as judges to oversee the competition. The event was a success and allowed each business to market its products in a way it had not before.

Volunteer with Purpose

This was the beginning of my experience of volunteering on purpose. If I could donate money to an organization in a meaningful way instead of using time away from my business, I made that choice. If I could offer experience in a way that the current volunteers could not for an organization, that was my choice. I wrote down my experiences and used them for a roadmap when volunteering:

- Entrepreneurship
- Marketing
- Speaking
- Leadership and mentoring

One evening I was invited to speak at the Junior League's joint council meeting. The setting was a large room of some of the most prolific volunteers in the community, high achievers in their own professions and thought leaders in regard to community activism. Their president had asked me, a fellow volunteer, to give a speech about female entrepreneurship.

This opportunity was amazing, but I felt like a complete fraud. My business that social media loved had a dirty little secret: it was a financial failure. However, I believed in entrepreneurship and loved that such a huge surge of female-owned businesses flooded the marketplace in recent years. I decided I would talk honestly about what I knew and how it had helped guide me in my venture.

Here is a shortened version of what I said at that meeting:

> Good evening.
>
> Female entrepreneurship is one of my biggest passions, and I'm excited to be here with you.
>
> In *4-Hour Workweek,* Tim Ferriss wrote, "An entrepreneur isn't someone who owns a business, it's someone who makes things happen."
>
> The entrepreneur mentality can be applied to many different areas, including our volunteer efforts, schools, church groups, and even home life.
>
> As I was pulling information to speak specifically about female entrepreneurs, I came across quotes saying you would never see the words "male entrepreneur." While I understand the statement, I have to say that right now is a very exciting time to be a woman in business.
>
> According to a *Forbes* article (now updated to reflect 2023 data), "There are currently around <u>252 million women entrepreneurs around the world</u>, and their

numbers have snowballed by 114% over the past two decades."

The number of female-owned businesses is on the rise across the United States, and I knew that I wanted to be one of them.

My background starts with a degree in journalism from the University of Oregon. I always had an entrepreneurial spirit but also wanted to be an actress telling a story through other voices. I built up my professional sales career while learning the art of acting. I led two parallel lives for a decade, but they never intersected.

Then I got married and started a family. Since I was married to a successful filmmaker, I chose to parent my kids on-location from various movie sites, and by the time we relocated to New Orleans, we had lived in five states and eight houses in three years. My career path had stopped completely, and although I loved being a mom more than anything, I was starting to lose my sense of self. My biggest challenge was I had an entrepreneurial spirit and wasn't sure how to utilize it.

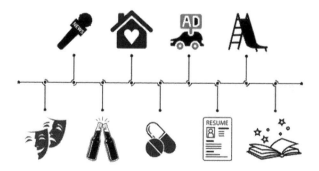

One day I sat down at my computer and wrote these words:

In my wallet I have a Screen Actors Guild card, an expired press pass, and a real estate broker's license. I sold beautiful, European-designed slipcovered furniture, worked for a major pharmaceutical company, and landed an account management job at a worldwide advertising agency. I served shots at an Irish pub, said a line to Scott Speedman in a Hollywood movie, and anchored the local news for a small cable channel.

In the ten years since graduating college, I have worked in seven different industries. I have three resumes and two demo tapes, depending on what type of interview I might have next.

I am ready to find an outlet for my intellectual and physical energy that will create an income for my family and fulfill my search for a professional identity that I have longed for since childhood.

One day I asked myself in bewilderment, Is it even possible to be professionally successful after so many years of failed attempts?

Then it occurred to me. I knew so many successful, professional women who have had challenges much more dramatic than I have been through, who now love their career paths. I decided to interview them. Maybe at least I would inspire myself, and hopefully I could inspire others. So that is what this writing work became: *Professional Women with Inspirational Stories.*

As the interviews commenced, I immediately noticed a commonality in this inspirational group. I realized that their chosen vocations were perfect in honoring their personas. These women did not define themselves by their jobs; their jobs were a reflection of their lifestyles and personalities.

After one year and many interviews, I found the answer to my initial question regarding the possibility of success after failure. More importantly, however, I realized that who I am is much more important than what I do.

The book was never completed because instead I wrote a business plan for Palm Tree Playground. However, many women I have spoken with describe a desire for a mentor, and I think that is what these women provided for me.

I thought it would be interesting to meet one of the entrepreneurs, a personal trainer named Kerry Rizzo, whom I worked with after my older daughter Madison was born. She had a training studio for new moms called After the Kids.

I remember her asking me, "This is your life. Is it what you want it to be?"

I told her that maybe I was never meant to find my calling, to which she responded, "Do you really think that is true?"

Kerry taught me that as women, we can have many true callings, including personal, professional, and spiritual ones, and that our hearts are capable enough to hold all of them. "Each moment writes your story. You are here for a reason right now in the perfect place."

Kerry went on to share with me, "My goal is to build women up physically, mentally, and spiritually. The only time I will ever have it all is when every woman in the world also has it all."

This leads me to the Palm Tree Playground story. I fell in love with an indoor playground in Portland, Oregon, called Play Boutique. I knew that I wanted to create something with the same feeling in New Orleans that was clean, friendly, safe, and fun. We immediately ran into serious challenges, but also fun successes.

The good outweighs the bad and we are anchored by an amazing team that understands our brand philosophy, and we support a community we dearly love.

I want to leave you with a note I received from a grandmother. Her daughter-in-law passed away in her sleep a week before her granddaughter's second birthday:

"Dear Heather, Thank you so much for your kindness and generosity on our granddaughter's second birthday. We were kind of at a loss as to how we could make her day special this year, but you were her guardian angel. We will always be grateful to you . . . Thank you, thank you, and God Bless."

This is why we created our business—community. Your simplest gift can be the biggest gift to someone else. Entrepreneurship has taught me how to meld business with humanity. Female business owners are poised to change the world. We just have to start.

Thank you for inviting me here tonight.

The exercise of writing this speech made me realize that when you share your story authentically, it, too, can be an act of service. Through my mistakes, I was able to craft an entrepreneurial story and share that with a group of women I felt were my superiors, and yet they thanked me after the evening and told me how much they had learned.

We all can volunteer in ways that are unique to us that change the communities we live in and thereby change the world around us. Time, money, and influence are different categories of volunteerism. Finding the balance amongst these opportunities to serve others can create deep joy and purpose in our lives. Having parameters to what we will say yes and no to gives freedom to not be stressed when asked to do something we do not feel is in alignment with our current season. The goal of volunteering is to be of service as long as possible and not to burn out after one particular season or event.

<u>Secret Start-Up Steps for Today</u>:

Answer the following questions:

1. What moves you emotionally in a way you would want to volunteer your time and talents to help serve?
2. What are your natural talents and gifts?

3. Is there something related to your business that you can donate to your community?

Take Action

Implement the Secret Start-Up Steps with the help of your free bonus bundle at heatherhays.co/book

We all can volunteer in ways that are unique to us that change the communities we live in and thereby change the world around us.

Secret Eight

SELF-CARE IS GOOD BUSINESS

You Don't Want the Urgent Matter to Be *You*

I was so happy I got my first mammogram at thirty-nine. I was ahead of schedule and ready to take forty on with enthusiasm. When my annual exam the next year revealed an early breast cancer diagnosis, I was literally shocked and knew I needed to implement immediate changes.

If you don't care for your body, you can't care for your business. There will always be another email, client request, or urgent matter, but if you continuously put yourself off, you might become the emergency someday. In five years, I gained fifty pounds running this business.

Self-care is good business. I had to stop compartmentalizing my life. Deprivation in one area of my life didn't add to richness in another. You are the CEO: invest in yourself and your health to go the distance with your business.

We know intellectually that exercise, sleep, nutrition, stress management, nature, and hobbies help care for our emotional and physical health. But when you are over-scheduled and feel like you have no time, where do you start? How do you put the phone down and allow yourself the thirty-minute walk?

Unfortunately, I never did and had serious consequences. I am not going to blame all my health issues on this business. However, I do believe my poor habits contributed to them, and once I changed my habits, my life changed for the better.

When we started PTP, I was working out daily and ate mostly gluten- and dairy-free. During the start-up phase, I stopped both of these practices, opting for a bagel and cream cheese at a coffee shop with my laptop instead of my normal gym morning. Once we opened the business, I stopped eating altogether and had never been thinner as an adult. I literally didn't think I had time to stop and eat. Looking back at this experience, I see that it was unacceptable. Simple meal prep would have solved this, and yet I didn't find the time because I was doing too much. I wanted to be the perfect stay-at-home/working mom/wife.

A few years later I had a stage 0 cancer diagnosis, and for a brief moment I wondered if I even needed to deal with it. Some women live with DCIS for years and nothing remarkable happens to their health. However, I had two parents who had experienced horrific cancer diagnoses, and I considered myself blessed to have an opportunity to deal with this one.

My decision at the time was to undergo a nine-hour surgery with reconstruction, which meant for six weeks, I would be out of the office for the majority of the time. While I was recovering, I thought about the years of sleep deprivation, sugar consumption to combat fatigue, and lack of exercise. I realized I had made everyone else's lives more important than mine. There wasn't one area of my life where I would delay a response to take care of my basic needs, like go to bed or attend a barre class. Change needed to take place, but I wasn't sure where to start.

As much as I would love to say that within a year of my surgery I had lost the fifty pounds and all my blood work normalized, I can't because it's not the truth. All of the quick-fix diet plans, cleanses, and thirty-day challenges didn't work for me. The issues were deep-rooted, and what worked for my friends didn't seem to work for me. Slowly, however, I met goals by making little changes and honoring the successes I did achieve. Today, for the first time in years, I am on a healing trajectory, and I have never felt better as an adult. Here is what I have learned:

12 Ideas to Get Healthier Today

- You are an amazing person no matter what the mirror reflects or scale measures.
- Real change takes time, and taking time creates lasting results.
- Starting slow is still starting. Commit to a thirty-minute walk a few times a week. Track the walk as a success. Once you have the walking down, find an additional

activity you enjoy. Have you always wanted to garden? Buy a few gardening tools and a pot. Learn how to sail, take a barre class, or join a walking group. It's amazing how you build community with activities you enjoy that create health practices.
- Momentum is precious. Once it gets going, protect it. Don't be shy about sharing your momentum with others. If you get asked to do something, you can say things like, "I would love to meet you for coffee after I get my workout completed."
- Buy a huge water bottle and drink filtered water all day long.
- Find a simple green juice recipe that doesn't require a juicer and drink it daily.
- When you are starting out, talk to your doctor or find a nutritionist to recommend some basic vitamins that we can't get from our food sources.
- Make one of your daily meals the prettiest salad you have ever seen. Prep all the ingredients for the week so you can be ready to go.
- If you take a daily prescription pill, buy a pill dispenser so you don't forget to take it or double up accidentally.
- Aim for eight hours of sleep. Those emails will wait, and if it's an emergency, you will

be called. Set that up in advance. Let your community know that after this particular hour, you are unavailable for health reasons.
- Sit in nature for a few minutes a day with your bare feet and hands on the grass or sand. This is called grounding, and it feels amazing.
- Consider talking to a therapist or counselor if you feel anxious or depressed.

Know that taking care of your needs benefits your spouse, partner, children, friends, family, investors, and team. You are not letting anyone down by caring about yourself. In fact, you are helping them take care of themselves by leading as a wonderful example.

Secret Start-Up Steps for Today:

1. What is one good health habit you can start today?
2. What is one habit you can start thinking about giving up to make healthier choices?
3. If you could pick a hobby you have always wanted to try, what would it be?

Take Action

Implement the Secret Start-Up Steps with the help of your free bonus bundle at heatherhays.co/book

If you don't care for your body, you can't care for your business.

Secret Nine

INVEST IN YOURSELF: FIND A MENTOR, SALES TRAINING, OR ENTREPRENEURSHIP PROGRAM

Why You Need a Mentor, Training, or Program

This chapter could be a part of Secret 3, You Are Not Alone, but I wanted it to stand out separately because investing in yourself is so vitally important for growth. You need a mentor, training, or program to develop yourself in areas that do not come naturally to you. Everyone learns from someone, and it's important that the people we choose to emulate align with our values and goals. Just like there are professionals to partner with to run your business, there are teachers, consultants, and learning programs to help you obtain skills that expand your knowledge and differentiate you from the competition. No one can take away a skill you have learned or a certificate you have earned. Education, growth, and upward trajectory attract a higher-level lifestyle in all areas, and you will never regret the time you spent preparing to be a better version of yourself.

January 2015

"Congratulations on your acceptance to Cohort 10 of Goldman Sachs 10,000 Small Businesses class at Delgado Community College! During orientation we will work together to establish a strong community of peer learning, explain the program's structure and expectations, and begin to frame your leadership and strategic growth efforts for the duration of the program."

Getting accepted into the Goldman Sachs 10,000 Small Businesses program with a curriculum designed by Babson College, the nation's top-ranked school for entrepreneurship, was my catalyst for change. The twelve-week course would culminate in a growth plan that would hopefully save my business. I felt incredibly lucky I had secured one of the spots in the 10th Cohort for the New Orleans location. This free program is offered around the county in person and online. The business owners who graduate from the course enjoy larger profits, a rich community of peers, and access to the best in practice entrepreneurial lessons available. For more information about the program and to learn if you qualify to apply, please visit: www.10ksbapply.com/

When I walked into the classroom on the first day surrounded by fellow business owners, I knew I was elevating myself with knowledge. In just the first three hours of class, a sense of community grew that only comes from being around like-minded people. Not only can you learn from the curriculum and teachers, but your entrepreneurial colleagues are invaluable.

You can do this by participating in an online mastermind group, hiring a coach, meeting with peers in your community, or even listening to fantastic podcasts that target topics you want to learn. The strategy for success is learning from individuals who already have the knowledge you want to obtain. It's smart business to realize you don't have all of the answers and to learn from others. There are invaluable courses and coaches that range from free to tens of thousands of dollars. There are mentors who can answer your questions and want to teach you how to succeed.

There are numerous options, and here is the best part: they are all waiting for you.

I wanted to learn how to have a growth mindset, and therefore working on a growth plan with experts was beneficial to me. That's why I was so confused when this happened on one of the first days:

"We are going to start by planning your exit strategy," the professor said. I was immediately confused. *Exit strategy* to me meant I would no longer be in business, and I had signed up for this program to learn how to successfully run my business with new strategies and practices. What I didn't understand yet was that when you run your business like you're going to sell it, you implement procedures and processes that can be duplicated with your team so the business owner can work on the business and not inside of it. This knowledge also makes it possible to create a franchise or multiple locations.

The growth plan is similar to a business plan, but because you have already been in business for two years, you are taking actual data and working with historical numbers and real-life circumstances.

When I wrote my business plan, it was all theory. When you write your growth plan, it is reality.

You aren't wishing for something to happen a certain way; you are reflecting on facts, and there is a huge amount of power in that. I loved being in the classroom. I enjoyed my growth group, and at times, I thought being included with peers who were so remarkable was the highest form of flattery to our business.

My favorite takeaways from the program:

- Entrepreneurship classes are very different from the business classes I experienced in the past.
- I already had so much available to me that I didn't realize. The list-building sessions of current assets that were not related to finances opened my eyes to a new reality.
- Owners must run a business as if they were going to sell it.
- I realized that the challenges I faced were similar to those of other small business owners and that I was not alone in my hurdles.
- Working "on" my business and not "in" my business was transformational.

Over the course of twelve weeks, the training changed the trajectory of our business and allowed us to sell when the timing was right. Palm Tree Playground was easier to run utilizing additional apps introduced in the course, including online scheduling tools, camp registrations, and social media platforms, that were inexpensive and simple to use. Additionally, we expanded our products and services in ways we never considered previously. We designed a summer camp for a new revenue stream and found ways to save money and make more money. We also applied for a line of credit from a banker who spoke as a guest, and we got it—all in a short three-month period.

As I wrote in my growth plan, "I applied for this program because of my belief in our product and my understanding of what our clients need. The process has changed me from an overwhelmed business 'worker' to an empowered business 'owner.' I feel optimism in the place of hopelessness and excitement where there was once fear."

How Sales Training Can Help You

Today learning has never been easier. Most topics are available for entrepreneurs via podcasts or for the price of a book, while some topics will require seasoned professionals to assist you. The important thing is to decide that you need help and then define what you need help with. What information are you seeking that would fill the gap between where you are and what your goals are?

The following are some ideas of what you might want to focus on, to get you started:

- Learning your leadership style and then creating professional processes to support that style.
- Creating new revenue streams with products and services that complement your current business.
- Reducing expenses by learning the art of negotiation by reviewing current contracts that are not serving you at their price points.
- Learning management tips that create accountability, reduce your stress, and inspire your team.
- Identifying key factors that promote and impede your growth.

- Producing a resource bank where you categorize everything you already have access to regarding human resources, networks, technology, organizations, financial, and physical property.
- Learning what your potential risks are and how you can safeguard yourself against them.
- Analyzing your financial reports with a professional to understand your true bottom line.
- Learning how to forecast your sales.
- Defining your marketing activities and determining their success.

Overcoming "I Don't Have Time"

There is a fair chance that if you are running a business and a life, you simply don't have time for one more thing. You might feel that the extra hour of learning could be committed to sleep or the extra dollar to an expense. I have been there and I understand that thought process.

Here is the bottom line:

You are worth the time it takes to learn a new skill.

You are worth the money invested to grow your plan.

While writing this book and learning to self-publish, I listened to numerous podcasts while walking for exercise (and lost twenty-five plus pounds). When I committed to the Goldman Sachs program, I decided it was worth the price to hire extra staff to cover the shifts I usually worked because I wanted to be an owner who looked at the big picture, not performed the daily details.

What will it take for you to begin your journey of investing in yourself with training that can level up your current situation? What free training is available to you in your community? What small steps can you make today?

I have a daughter who attends a school forty-five minutes away from our house. I decided that after I dropped her off, I would only listen to podcasts about personal development. That drive that seemed "so far" in the beginning and could have been a negative, eventually turned into a huge positive and a stepping stone to my new career.

Investing in yourself with education, coaching, reading a book, or listening to a podcast becomes time spent building your future success.

Secret Start-Up Steps for Today:

Answer the following questions:
1. What opportunities for entrepreneurship learning do you have in your community?
2. What is one area of growth you want to strengthen?
3. Is there a coach or program you want to learn more about to help you effectively invest in yourself? Perhaps explore a new podcast or business book if you don't know where to start.

Take Action

Implement the Secret Start-Up Steps with the help of your free bonus bundle at heatherhays.co/book

You will never regret the time you spent preparing to be a better version of yourself.

Secret Ten

YOU CAN (SOMETIMES) SELL A BUSINESS THAT ISN'T PROFITABLE

How to Find a Buyer for Your Business

Five years into parties, playdates, and countless memories, my husband and I realized we had to either sell the business or close it. This was an incredibly hard decision, but the cash flow we needed to make this a long-term venture was not materializing, and I needed to shift my energy to something that would. If you research how to sell your business, you will find that most sources say you must show profits for at least two years before the sale. Consultants instruct you to increase sales to motivate buyers. Of course, that was the plan, but it was not working.

After speaking with a business broker who was, not surprisingly, very unimpressed with our numbers, I knew the standard listing process would not be successful and contemplated closing at the end of the month.

I knew I would be sad with whatever decision we came to, but what I didn't count on was our team's reaction.

The managers who had been with us since opening day were devastated. Their eyes instantly filled with tears that soon would run down their cheeks as they mourned the first jobs they had with a team that was literally family. One of the managers spoke to her father-in-law, who ran multiple businesses, about the possibility of running Palm Tree Playground under new ownership.

We couldn't show large profits, so what could we show? Could we really sell a business that wasn't producing consistent income? How do you sell a business that's unsellable according to a majority consensus?

In our case, the answer was we had to find the right buyer. We had to find someone who saw value in our business model, inventory, location, investments, name, email list, and reputation. There was an intrinsic value to Palm Tree

Playground that could be monetized with the right buyer. For us, that buyer was someone with the following characteristics:

- Emotionally invested in the business through current employees.
- Able to see a potential for increased sales with the base we had built.
- Interested in the value of the brand's reputation in the community.
- Confident that the business could run with the current management in place and that our systems, and not us as the owners, were integral to our success.

Information Requested by Potential Buyers

To determine if this was a viable investment opportunity, our buyer wanted to ensure the day-to-day operations would not be an out-of-pocket cost to him and that he would not have to work in the business at all. Ascertaining that his goals were possible took many conversations between him and his family who already worked at our facility. In addition, he needed data from us that included the following:

- Sales data: By utilizing our ShopKeep App, we had data from the last five years to share in organized reports.

- Expenses: Thanks to our Quicken program, we could share the monthly expenses, including payroll, effortlessly.
- Future party bookings: We ran Party Centre Software reports for every future event and deposit on the schedule.
- Copy of waiver our clients signed upon entry to the facility.
- Merchant account records
- Lease
- Repair estimates

The new owner wanted to leave all of the management and processes in place. He was only going to reduce expenses by using suppliers he already worked with. He wanted to ensure that my team was solid and could work without me at the helm. Fortunately, we had already committed to the following years earlier:

- Running PTP as efficiently as possible with every process written up in an easily organized and utilized manner.
- Fully training our team and having a new-hire process in place.
- Having finances in order with all accompanying documents, including tax returns.
- Ensuring the POS system software was up-to-date.

- Completing our customer database with all pertinent information including a healthy email list with thousands of names.
- Keeping records of all upcoming business-related events that required deposits paid to our company.
- Keeping inventory lists of equipment, merchandise, and supplies.

Combining all of this information formed a package for the buyer that convinced him to purchase the business. We had a wonderful transition of ownership, and to this day I am so grateful we were able to sell Palm Tree Playground and not close it.

Life After the Business Sale

The day we sold Palm Tree Playground, I thought I would feel something like grief when I handed over my keys. I did not, I felt light. After five years, I realized I had brought the business into the world but didn't need to run it. I had created something that now had a life of its own. Maybe that was a success in itself?

With the financial stress gone immediately, I was able to shift my thinking from fear based to reflective. The business we had created as a team and community offered light and love in a world where destruction and chaos thrive. There is great honor in trying something and pouring your heart into it without a guarantee. Palm Tree Playground invested hundreds of thousands of dollars into the local economy and community, offering wonderful people jobs. We were honored to celebrate hundreds of children and their birthdays alongside their families. The business was integrated into the community and became a valuable resource. And finally, I used my knowledge to volunteer and create other business opportunities for female entrepreneurs through organizations like the Junior League of New Orleans and New Orleans Entrepreneur Week.

You, too, can make a list of all the positives that might have come out of something that didn't feel like a success. I urge you to write those accomplishments and milestones down in a journal and remind yourself that each one of these things means something to not only you but also your circle.

About six months after the sale of the Palm Tree Playground, I had to pick something up from our old manager. Our daughters' tiny handprints could still be seen embedded into what looks like sand around the playground. There were adorable toddlers playing in the enclosed three-and-under area that looked like a small beach park. Moms were gathered in the cafe, sipping hot coffee and relaxing into new friendships they'd made through the kinship of parenthood.

I honored the creativity and work it took to turn a motorcycle dealership into the #1 children's indoor playground year after year as voted in the top family magazine in town.

This was not the way this dream was supposed to end, but thankfully, selling the business so that it could still thrive and move forward allowed me to move on too.

The entrepreneurial spirit doesn't break. It might fade for a bit and reflect on the sting, but what comes next is always better. You can change the narrative, sell the unsellable start-up, and begin again.

Secret Start-Up Steps for Today:

Answer the following questions:

1. Are you interested in selling your business one day?
2. What data would you need to prepare that you don't already collect to make that sale viable?
3. What intrinsic value does your business offer? How can you build on that?

Take Action

Implement the Secret Start-Up Steps with the help of your free bonus bundle at heatherhays.co/book

The entrepreneurial spirit doesn't break. It might fade for a bit and reflect on the sting but what comes next is always better.

CONCLUSION

Today, I am writing this to you from my new backyard, overlooking the Pacific Ocean in Honolulu, Hawaii. It's been eleven years, to the day, from opening those old Honda dealership doors where I created my start-up indoor playground. Our family lives close to the beach, surrounded by plumeria and palm trees, all with an expansive view of blue waters during the day and orange sunsets at night. I quite literally live in a palm tree playground.

I finished this book after years of contemplation and writing. When I started, there was no Palm Tree Playground, of course. My book idea was about professional authenticity.

My goal was to write a book about professional women with inspirational stories. I had a list of entrepreneurs who shared their time with me and took me through their own professional wins and losses. The women were vastly different from each other. Some have gone on to become extremely successful household names, and one was even featured on the *Today Show*. Others gave up on their dreams completely. If I had written that book, it would have only been a snapshot in time of their story. I love the quote by Orson Welles, "If you want a happy ending, that depends of course, on where you stop your story."

To be fully authentic, I decided I had to give you a full story, and I couldn't do that by just giving you a peek into other women's journeys that provided the perfect conclusions.

These are my own successes and failures to share. I truly believe career transition requires inspiration and that anything you desire is possible. I believe in professional optimism. I believe you can work your current job as a source of income and fulfill your passion through outside interests. More importantly, however, I believe that who I am is much more important than what I do, because it affects all areas of my life. The job doesn't create me; I create the job, the possibilities, and the future. And if one path doesn't work, it's only because another one is waiting that's better.

Many entrepreneurs do not go to business school but instead are creative thinkers who are innovative and fill a gap in the marketplace when others are too scared to do so. It might be smart to only run a business if you have a business degree, but then I think we might miss out on some of the world's greatest products.

When we are authentic in what we do and create a product we truly believe in, we are successful. I now realize that Palm Tree Playground was a success in that it delivered on a promise of high quality parties and playtime to our youngest guests and their families.

Your product or service has the power to change people's lives. I hope these ten start-up secrets can be a solid platform from which you launch your newest dream or product or redesign an existing one. The Business Diaries was written to empower, encourage and energize female entrepreneurs just like you to transform your business and lifestyle. Here's to your future endeavors!

When we are authentic in what we do and create a product we truly believe in, we are successful.

Made in the USA
Middletown, DE
04 April 2024